10 Steps to Find Work and Be Successful in Canada

A Guide for Immigrants Who Want To Thrive In a New Culture

By: Gabriela M Radix

Table of Contents

Introduction

According to the inaugural list of the world's best countries, Canada was ranked as the second best country in the world. It is peaceful, friendly and beautiful and on top of this is still accepting new immigrants.

When you are accepted and get ready to come to Canada, you are excited, full of hopes and everything sounds like a sweet dream. Soon after you land, your experience might change. For many new immigrants the adventure transforms into a nightmare as they face the hard reality of the competitive Canadian labour market.

For entry level jobs such as customer service, cashier, or flipping burgers there are from 120 to over 200 applications. Can you imagine? Current statistics in North America say that it can take up to six months to one year to land a good job.

While that seems daunting, there is hope!

Before looking for work, it is important to understand the competition and the employer's needs. By doing this, you'll be able to target your search and learn how to separate yourself from the many other applicants.

Your competition for these jobs is varied. Students from all over the world come to study in Canada and decide to stay here and make a living, qualified and experienced immigrants who already have Canadian experience and are looking for another job, native Canadians who lived their entire life in this country and have a solid professional and social network. And other new immigrants like you, who are looking for the same opportunities.

In a free labour market, when the government is still accepting skilled workers but doesn't provide or guarantee work for them, you need to start relying on yourself.

After reading this guide you will know where to go, what to do, and how to look for work and be successful in a much shorter time.

This book is an interactive and resourceful guideline for immigrants; "new or old" or just on their way here, who want to achieve success in Canada and is a must read if you want to take the lead in your job search and be successful.

In this book you will learn from the experiences of successful immigrants in Canada and their job search secrets, experts in the field and the newest trends in the job market, road maps for self-discovery, job search resources and great tips on how to sell yourself, get interviews and land successful jobs in the Canadian market.

You deserve an amazing life and career. Let's get started!

Chapter 1 - Available and Free Resources

So you are new in town, time to get a job!

A big majority of newcomers start by applying online right away. If you already tried this and you weren't successful it means that you are doing something wrong and you should change the process.

There are free resources provided by the government that you might not be aware of because you don't have similar services in your home country.

1. **Employment Centers**

Among the most useful of these are Employment Centers; which can help job seekers to find employment.

These facilities provide information about community resources, colleges and programs related to your interests, work opportunities, and funding if you qualify.

They also have workshops on career exploration and job search. For somebody new in country and not familiar with Canadian culture, labour market trends, employers 'needs, and job searching skills this is a must.

All the services are free. On top of this you can connect with employers at hiring fairs, receive direct job leads from your caseworker, network with other job seekers, create a support system and make new friends.

2. <u>English Second Language Classes</u>

If your English level needs to be improved, ESL classes are the solution. It might take some time to get into a class but you'll get there eventually.

English Second Language (ESL) programs are designed for specific skill levels, groups of learners and specific purposes. There are many organizations that provide these classes.

3. <u>Provincial Programs</u>

There are many other initiatives, local programs, and funding available dedicated to helping immigrants with settlement and integration in Canada. The best way is to go to the closest Employment Center and ask about services available for new immigrants. You are considered a new immigrant if you have less than 5 years since you moved to Canada.

You can also check the government website for Canada Immigration and Citizenship and all the information about programs available. It is a great resource for many people who need to keep abreast of all the latest trends, opportunities and initiatives.

CIC - http://www.cic.gc.ca/english/

As I said, the first step is to check all the resources available for free. I know many people who came to Canada years ago when these benefits did not exist and their path was much harder than ours is today.

After moving here, I took advantage of everything that was available at that time. I attended a few governmental programs that allowed me to get familiar with Canadian culture and gain clarity about what wanted to do here. I was able to meet 'friends for life' and find mentors who guided me along the process.

All the free resources I benefited from helped me to shape my way and first job in Canada.

Chapter 2 - A New Beginning

'Choose a job you love, and you will never have to work a day in your life' – Confucius

Sometimes in workshops I ask clients to tell me how many hours / days /months /years they are going to work for the rest of their life. The average person spends 90,000 hours at work over their lifetime and more than 80% of people are dissatisfied with their jobs.

Is it worth it to waste it and feel miserable every day? The game of life should be fun, not a burden as you end up spending more time working than with your family or enjoying life.

I recommend you to start immediately questioning yourself:

- Why did you choose your profession?
- When do you feel useful and have a feeling of fulfilment?
- What do you enjoy doing that makes you lose track of time?

Most of the people who are passionate about their jobs know why they enjoy it. They don't feel that they need to sell themselves for the job, they just talk with passion and interest about what they enjoy doing.

You might not always have the right words to describe it but if you have a genuine smile on your face while you are talking about your passion you will easily learn how to create a personal brand and market your skills.

When you are coming here you might consider these options:

1. Choose a different career
2. You climb back to your old profession
3. You become an entrepreneur and start you own business

No matter what path you choose please remember that coming to Canada is also a new beginning to exploring new career opportunities and passions.

Chapter 3 - Find out What Employers Want

I found that one of the common and big obstacles to getting hired sooner is to stay focused on what worked for you back home and on what you want from a job. We simply make too many assumptions and we forget the most important thing that needs to be taken into consideration – the needs of the employer and what they are looking for in an employee.

When you apply with a four-page resume and mention all the technical skills and qualifications you have and nothing about the kind of person you are, employers don't actually get to know you very well. And employers have lots of fears around hiring somebody who they don't know and trust.

Employers might be afraid:

- That you don't understand all the job requirements
- It might take you longer to acclimate and do the job as they expect
- You will refuse to adapt in a new culture and will make everyone in the team feel uncomfortable by imposing your beliefs, culture, traditions, and habits
- They will spend resources to train you and you will not stay for a long time

Going back to employers. What do they want? What does it take to get a job in Canada? Please stop making assumptions.

It's time to find out. There are three primary things an employer wants an employee to do.

1. **To fix their problems**

   You are hired because they need somebody to help them with their business. If they don't have any need then you are not hired.
   Every employer is looking for a specific set of skills from job-seekers that match the skills necessary to perform a particular job.

   Work related skills are known as either technical or hard skills. Most of the time these skills are easy to measure, such as typing speed, driving a forklift, lifting, and blueprint reading.

2. **To be a good fit**

   They are looking for a unique combination of skills and values that will make you fit in a pre-existing team.

   They are looking for somebody who matches their own values and image of a good employee.

3. **To be self-directed**

You need to know how to do the job, but beyond these job-specific technical skills they want somebody with a great personality and attitude. These attributes are known as soft skills.

It is not that technical skills and knowledge aren't important. The truth is that technical skills can be taught more easily than soft skills, which tend to be either personal characteristics or skills that have been fine-tuned over a period of time.

Opposite to hard skills, the soft skills are always transferable but hard to measure. Examples of soft / transferable skills: are communication, being a team player, resourceful, and showing initiative. The best part is that these skills can be acquired in any life setting so they are not necessarily related your job.

According to a recent study in 2015 by Workopolis Canadian employers want to hire more people but they struggle to find the right candidates with the skills that they need.

What do Canadian employers say candidates are lacking?

- Experience – 38%

- Soft skills – 29%

- Technical skills – 23%

- Education – 4%

Looking at those numbers, it is clear employers are looking for on-the-job experience, and that soft skills out-weigh the technical

Chapter 4 - Identify your Soft Skills (Transferable Skills)

Shortly after I came here I learned about transferable skills and how can I transfer those skills from engineering to coaching; or facilitating. It was my "aha" moment and my biggest realization about how I can be successful in Canada. What I learned changed the way I communicated with people, the way I pursued my job hunting and all the relationships that I have built here.

This can be difficult for people coming from Europe and Asia where education and technical skills are what matter the most for employers. If you are an expert in your field, you can get along just fine if you don't have the most pleasant personality. Being knowledgeable, having many years of experience in the field, or a higher degree, like a Master's, or PHD is what would get you hired.

In North America though, employers want to see more than that. They want to see that you have soft skills. This is what actually will get you hired here.

Transferable skills can be used in many different types of jobs. They are personal qualities and attitudes that can help you to work well with others and make a positive contribution to organisations you work for.

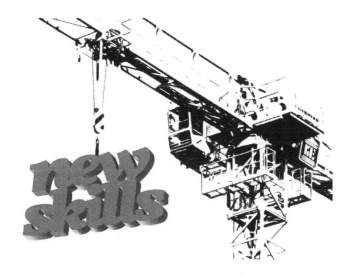

Here is a list of the most valued soft skills by employers:

- Communication
- Problem Solving
- Organizing
- Decision making
- Loyalty
- Flexibility
- Time management
- Team player
- Leadership
- Accountability

Now let's focus on the most important of them and apply them to our situation. After each skill you have examples of a **skills statement** that you can use in your resume, cover letter or interviews.

Communication

This covers verbal communication, writing, and listening skills.

The ability to communicate clearly and being able to tailor your message for the audience and listening attentively to others. Communication also includes the ability to follow directions and provide feedback.

Let's be honest! As immigrants, English pronunciation and grammar might not be our best strength. Our advantage is that words are not the most important thing in the communication process. Instead, focus on body language and nonverbal communication. It is known that nonverbal communication it is way more powerful than just using words.

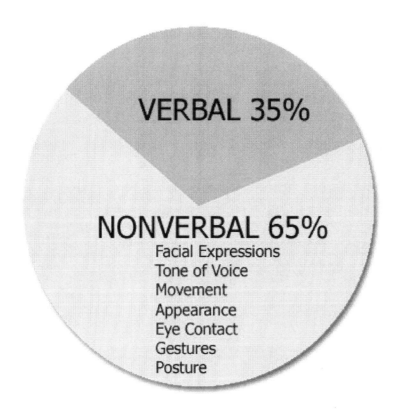

That is something that you can easily learn and practice by using:

- Eye contact

- Facial expressions

- Body movements, posture

- Gestures

- Touch

- Space

- Voice

It's not just what you say; it's how you say it. When I coach people for interviews I always start with body language. The most important factor in an interview is the first impression. That first impression is the sum of small signals given by: your body language and posture, handshake, smile, eye contact, the way you are dressed up, your voice, energy, hand gestures and so many other tiny things that we disregard most of the time

How you can you become a master of communication and a strong leader.

1. **Join a Toastmaster club**. There are many Toastmaster clubs that you can join and become a confident public speaker. There are also dedicated clubs for ESL people so you can improve your English and communication skills.

   Toastmasters have changed the lives of many immigrants by giving the opportunity to speak and receive constructive feedback. It also shapes your leadership skills and connects you with thousands of people.

In my first week after my arrival I checked out a Toastmaster club and joined shortly after. Today, I am still a member of this club and all can say is that I am sure that I wouldn't be a confident speaker today if I didn't make the decision to become a member.

2. **Communication Course**: There are many communication workshops that you can take and help you improve communication skills either in a group setting, online or one-on-one coaching session provided by a coach or personal trainer.

   Coming from different cultures we don't know the golden rules for communication in North America. As an example, employers here value direct eye contact as a sign of trust and respect. This is contrary to some other cultures in which direct eye contact means disrespect or arrogance. They also value a firm hand shake.

   If this is the number one skill wanted by any employer than I think that you should invest your time or money in becoming an effective communicator.

Examples of a communication skills statement

- Liaise and communicate effectively with team members and other professionals

- Able to build and maintain long lasting relationships with follow-up and keeping the lines of communication open with customers and partners

- Delivered Powerful Talks that consistently influenced more than 50% of customers to purchase products

- Established reputation for communicating with clarity and diplomacy to individuals from diverse cultural

Problem Solving

Employers are looking for people who are motivated to take on challenges with minimal direction and react accordingly when something needs to be done.

The moment you decide on applying to a specific company you need to find out what kind of problems they have.

Remember that if they don't have any problems they don't have any need to hire you!

You need to then identify how you can help the employer solve those problems.

Examples of a problem solving skills statement

One simple technique that you can use is:

The "I Help _____ do _____" Technique

"I help delivering goods to customers in a safe and timely manner"

"I help businesses achieve the breakthrough results they need"

"I help empower immigrants."

"I help people with language barriers to find their voice'

Organizational Skills

Prospective employees need to be able to prioritise, work efficiently and productively, and manage time well. This is actually what employers want to see on your resumes and hear in interviews.

Examples of an organization skills statement

- Strong planning and prioritization skills; manage time effectively to accomplish tasks

- Thorough and accurate recording of information and maintaining records

- Good organizational skills with proven ability to plan and prioritize tasks

- Prioritize workflow to ensure completion of accurate work within established deadlines

- Well organized, saved time by planning delivery travel schedules and service routes

Time management

Time is money. Time management is the ability to plan and manage multiple assignments and tasks and; set priorities while meeting deadlines. Time management skills help you to have a greater productivity and efficiency in any task you perform.

Examples of a time management skills statement

- Able to allocate time effectively, work under pressure and manage tight deadlines

- Excellent ability to prioritize tasks and multitask

- Strong background in analyzing processes and selecting the simplest way to accomplish a task

- Able to break up big projects into small and manageable parts

Making decisions

Are you a creative person able to think outside the box? Do you think on your feet? Do you use past experiences as valuable lessons to identify and solve problems effectively?

Employers want you to make sound judgements about what to do in a difficult situation when they are not present.

Examples of a making decision skills statement

- Evaluated the costs and benefits associated with each option

- Able to assess the impact of the decision and modify the course of action

  as needed

- Brainstormed and generated a list of name options for a new product

Loyalty and commitment

The word of the day is "trustworthy". Employers want to trust their employees to work professionally and represent the employer's best interests.

You are the image, the brand. For example, if you are working in any customer service job and you treat clients disrespectfully or you are getting in arguments with them (even if you are right), you risk dragging the company's name down and destroying their reputation. You might lose your job but they have much more to lose.

NEVER talk bad about your previous company, colleagues, customers...anyone. No matter what happens.

NEVER disclose anything negative about a previous employer. The employer interviewing you will likely think you'll do the same to them.

You can display loyalty through integrity.

Examples of a loyalty and commitment skills statement

- Recognized for 10 years of 'perfect attendance'
- Trusted for opening and closing the store in my first month of work

Flexibility, Adaptability and Availability

Business needs are changing all the time and employers expect you to react quickly to changing business conditions. Most jobs require flexibility regarding working hours, overtime, job duties or location.

Examples of a flexibility skills statement

- Willing to learn new methods, procedures or techniques and take on new tasks

- Able to work flexible hours including weekends and holidays

Team Player

Take any job posting and check for the word team player. Two of three job postings contain this word. Getting along with your colleagues, partners, and supervisors is an essential skill. Being a team player is about cultivating positive working relationships that help everyone to achieve goals and business objectives.

Examples of a team player skills statement

- Enjoy working as a team member as well as independently

- Thrive in a team environment and work well with others

- Independently motivated and driven while contributing in a team setting

- Defined common goals for projects

- Skilled in cultivating positive relationships with clients and colleagues

Leadership

Too many people feel confused and say that they never had a position as a leader and therefore they don't possess leadership skills or qualities. Hard to believe, but everyone has shown leadership skills in various situations by doing simple things like:

- Listening to a colleague who had a hard day
- Organizing an event (work, community)
- Motivating or inspiring somebody
- Jumping in a difficult situation, leading a team
- Being responsible for training new staff

Spend some time reflecting on your work history and you should easily be able to identify a situation when you showed leadership qualities.

Examples of a leadership skills statement

- Trained and mentored over 50 new staff

- Exceptional leadership skills championing performance improvement
- Demonstrated ability to influence, communicate effectively and build relationships

Accountability

Being on time, meeting deadlines, delivering quality of services are traits employers want to see. Making mistakes can happen as we are not robots but not taking responsibility for your mistakes or blaming others will make you lose the respect of others. Accept failures, learn the lessons and then find solutions for improvement.

Example of an accountability skills statement

- Responsible for handling large workloads in fast-paced environments

- Recognised for the ability to complete tasks on time

Other Skills

There are many other very important soft skills that you should have on your resume, in your cover letter, and ready to use in interviews. Researching, multitasking, working under pressure, safety, and creativity are just some of them.

But here is the trick. How can you add all of them in one or two pages' resume? Or talk about them in one minute or less in an interview?

The fact is, you can't. Focus on the most important soft skills required by the employers. These can be found by carefully reading the job posting and highlighting the most important ones that are relevant to the employer and job.

TIP: 80% of job seekers make one big mistake when using soft skills. They just list them. Whenever I ask people to tell me about their skills or strengths they enumerate them, letting me know that they are organized, reliable, punctual, honest, team player.

No one gains any value if you just enumerate a list of skills. This in not powerful and I assure you that employers are not impressed. Instead of doing that, create skills statements that show you understand what the skill is rather than simply knowing the word for it.

Chapter 5 - Make a list of Keywords and Power words

One secret to making a good impression on employers is if you use common words that are recognized in your industry and by employers. This will give them the impression that you speak the same language and you are one of them.

There is another main reason why it is so important to start using keywords. When you apply online with your resume there are two main ways used by that employer to read your resume:

1. Human Being (HB): A human resources representative, hiring manager, supervisor or any designated person in the hiring process.

2. Applicant Tracking System (ATS): This is an automated system used by employers to handle the recruitment process and scan and sort through thousands of resumes so they find the best fit for the company.

   They are looking for certain criteria and keywords that match the job requirement. If you misspelled words, or added irrelevant words that don't match the job posting the system will delete your resume.

The simplest way to identify keywords is to use the words from the job posting. Highlight the job requirements, verb phrases and skills required. Look also for words that are repeating or are bolded or are at the beginning or end of a paragraph.

You can also check the company's website and look for information about the company in the About Us or Mission / Values sections and write it down. Once you have identified the keywords, insert them in your resume and cover letter.

Let's take this Job Posting example.

Desired Skills and Experience - Production Engineer

- Mechanical Engineering Degree
- Minimum 2 years plant operating experience project engineering
- Training and hands-on experience in leadership, team development, time management, safety systems
- Excellent interpersonal and leadership skills
- Able to identify, solve, and implement solutions
- Excellent mechanical aptitude

This is just a piece of the job description but it gives us the opportunity to identify what are the top skills employer is looking for in this line of work and target my resume and cover letter

Step 1 - Highlight the keywords (What are the most important skills for employers?)

- **Mechanical Engineering Degree**
- Minimum 2 years **plant operating experience and project engineering**
- Training and hands-on experience in **leadership**, team development, **time management**, **safety** systems
- **Excellent interpersonal** and leadership skills
- Able to identify, **solve**, and implement solutions
- **Excellent mechanical aptitude**

Step 2 – Incorporate keywords in Resume Profile / Qualifications/Work Experience

- Creative thinker, demonstrated ability to effectively **solve** problems
- Able to troubleshoot and fix **mechanical** problems
- Experienced **Project Engineer**, able to analyze opportunities and determine the most beneficial path

- A great **communicator** who can tie together the needs of different working groups
- Enthusiastic Team Leader with 5+ years of proven track record of success in plant operation, management and **leadership**

Step 3 - Check the keywords for ATS screening

Use Job Scan for checking the Keywords – an application designed to help you compare your resume with the job posting you are applying for. All you need is to create a free account and upload the resume and a job posting and it will check how well your resume compares to a job (similar- ATS)

Job Scan - https://www.jobscan.co/

You can also use Wordle and TagCrowd to refine the selection of keywords. These resources help find recurring words (themes) on a website.

Wordle - http://www.wordle.net/

TagCrowd - http://tagcrowd.com/

Step 4 – Use powerful words and verbs

Action Verbs

- led
- managed
- trained
- mentored
- coached
- achieved
- demonstrated
- multiplied
- upgraded
- encouraged
- completed
- coordinated
- delegated
- advised
- allocated
- compiled

- calculated
- scheduled
- generated
- debugged
- reduced
- solved
- transformed
- delivered
- diagnosed
- evaluated
- forecasted
- negotiated
- prioritised
- addressed
- interpreted
- persuaded

- inspired
- motivated
- wrote
- envisioned
- fabricated
- identified
- shaped
- tailored
- presented
- facilitated
- guided
- mediated
- promoted
- reported
- resolved
- organised
- indicated
- displayed
- assisted
- participated
- contributed
- prepared
- performed
- operated
- served
- created
- designed
- implemented
- balanced
- increased
- improved
- executed

Descriptive word list / Personal attributes

- Genuine
- Dedicated
- Motivated
- Creative
- Enterprising
- Likeable
- Reliable
- Trustworthy
- Organized
- People-oriented
- Cooperative
- Loyal
- Supportive
- Professional
- Flexible
- Courageous

- Imaginative
- Dependable
- Intuitive
- Unique
- Independent
- Dynamic
- Open-minded
- Businesslike
- Calm
- Capable
- Visionary
- Persuasive
- Diligent
- Hardworking
- Effective
- Easygoing

- Helpful
- Kind
- Meticulous
- Observant
- Optimistic
- Patient
- Outgoing
- Energetic
- Self-Aware
- Analytical
- Thorough
- Warm
- Sharp

- Focused
- Innovative
- Approachable
- Cheerful
- Confident
- Determined
- Efficient
- Assertive
- Enthusiastic
- Savvy
- Resourceful
- Procedural
- Goal oriented

Chapter 6 - Developing compelling marketing tools: Resume and Cover Letter

Resume

"A resume good for everything is good for nothing". This is a principle that I learned the hard way as I applied for job after job and heard nothing back.

Like many of you, after I came here I submitted many resumes hoping to get a call back. It didn't happen, not even when I went in person. Why? Because it was a general resume, not targeting any specific job.

From engineering to customer service, it was not relevant to the job I was applying for. It was a three-page Resume with spelling mistakes and not well formatted. And I wondered why I didn't get a call back.

You don't need to be a resume expert but you need to create a unique resume that reflects your best strengths and is relevant to the job.

As a job coach, I run many resume workshops and the question I always begin with is "What is the purpose of the resume?"

The answers always the same:

"To sell ourselves."

"To talk about our skills and what can we do for the employer."

"To get a job."

There is nothing wrong with these answers; except they miss the main purpose of the resume - *to get you an interview*! A piece of paper will not get you a job. Maybe a call back and after that an interview.

Choose your Resume Style

In resume writing, there are different styles of resumes styles and formats. Each style is unique on its own and it's up to you to choose the right style of resume.

Functional Resume

A functional resume contains a list of your skills and work experience which are sorted by job function or skill area. A functional resume is never used to focus on experiences and skills that are specific to the job you sought.

 Functional resume directly utilizes experience summaries and emphasizes specific professional abilities as the means of presenting your professional competency.

Chronological Resume

The Chronological Resume style is the most common resume style and preferred by employers.
This style of resume lists your job experiences in chronological order, hence the name. It commonly covers your experience for the previous years and is used mostly when you are specialised and have lots of experience in one filed.

The positions that you have are listed along with beginning and ending dates. In case of current positions, starting date to "present" or the "current year" is put instead of the ending date.

Combined Resume

This style fuses the approach of both the functional resume and chronological resume style. Combined resume is composed of a functional list of your job skills that is followed by the list of your employers in a chronological order. Unfortunately, combined resume it can repeat itself, thus it's less used compared to the previous two styles from which it was derived.

Video & website Resume

If you feel creative and willing to play the big game take advantage of the multimedia power of the internet. Shifting to info graphics, videos, and websites are now trending. Despite the increasing trend, this style attracted criticisms from human resource professionals. A large number of recruiters out there still prefer the traditional resume format.

Online Resume

Since employers now find potential applicants through the use of search engines it is important to use proper keywords in writing resumes. Employers find it convenient to use Applicant Tracking Systems because they can save time by filtering high volumes of resumes instead of sorting massive stacks of paper.

You can upload your resume in Microsoft Word, but some employers also require PDF or HTML. If you have choice between Microsoft Word and PDF, choose PDF as can be valuable if you have spelling mistakes.

After choosing your resume style, let's focus on structure and the content of a resume.

1. The first important aspect is the length.

One or two pages is enough. Even if you are a professional and have twenty years of experience you don't need to write *everything* you've ever done on one resume. Your resume should target just the relevant experience to the job and make the employer curious and interested about you. The focus is on quality and not quantity.

2. Structure of the resume

- Name - contact information – address
- Objective
- Profile or Summary of Qualifications
- Work Experience and /or Volunteer Experience
- Education and training

1. Name - Contact information - Address

Name: A recent study in Canada says that your name will impact a call back.

An employer will often feel embarrassed if a name is hard to pronounce and will avoid calling you; and if you do get hired, you can still run into this problem with fellow employees and customers.

One strategy that we can adopt is to "change our name" in the resume as it is not a legal document. We can use a nick name, English name or abbreviation for your legal name that is easy for employers to pronounce it. Once you have the interview you can introduce yourself with your legal name.

Address: Avoid including your full address. There are many scams on Craigslist and other job sites and some people are taken advantage of on social media channels. Stating the city and province should be enough.

Email: Email addresses present problems similar to those with difficult to pronounce names. I've had many clients coming with email addresses and names from their home countries.
They need to sound Canadian. Here, employers prefer you using Gmail or outlook accounts. If they see your email address from a different country or with an unusual name, they might not even open it due to fears of internet scams or accidently downloading a virus

TIP: Use your first and last name in your email address. Avoid adding numbers like your age, year of birth, or current year as it gives the impression that you are brand new to computers.

If you have a nice and professional LinkedIn account, you can include it in your resume.

2. Objective

Most of the employers prefer you to "Ditch the Career Objective Statement". The reason is because most of the time it can be used to screen you out for focusing on your own goals: "I am looking for a job".

The resume needs to be short and to the point and the first statement has to pull the employer's attention in from the start and give them a reason to continue reading. You can include an objective statement that stands out from the crowd and position it as a title or a subtitle in your Profile.

3. Profile or Summary of Qualifications

The profile is the most important part of your resume. In maybe less than fifteen seconds they will scan your resume and make a decision about it. As a result, if you don't have a *powerful* profile your resume will end up in the garbage! Any job seeker who wants to be successful and receive a call back needs to put in the effort and build a powerful profile.

This is why it is important to start with soft and hard skills. Once you are able to identify the skills that you have and the employers' needs we can start designing the resume.

The truth is that you can't sell yourself if you don't have any idea of what can you offer. The "please give me a job" attitude is not working in this labour market.

Here is the formula for building a powerful profile:

- years of experience in your field
- education, qualification, training
- hard skills, knowledge of
- hard skills expertise, proficiency in
- soft skills (communication, languages, organization,)
- soft skills (leadership, flexibility, team work, etc)
- achievement

Let's look at how this structure is applied in a customer service profile

Profile / Summary of Qualifications

- More than five years of experience providing stellar customer service

- Serving it Right certificate, training in conflict resolution
- Able to operate all types of cash registers with a high degree of accuracy
- Skilled in developing and delivering customer center solutions
- Excellent organizational skills; able to prioritize and complete tasks on schedule
- Effective communicator: successfully de-escalated customers' complaints ensuring future business and customer satisfaction
- Fluent in English and Hindi
- Received positive feedback from guests for consistently meeting their needs

If you follow this simple structure for your resume I guarantee that your luck will change!

TIP: Do you want to have an outstanding resume?

One important think to keep in mind when you build your resume profile is that the first and last 2 bullet points are the most important. This is what employers will remember the most. So make sure that your best strengths are emphasised in the first and last bullet points.

Another way to give your resume more punch is to use numbers. They can be used to showcase the scope and scale of your responsibilities as well as your accomplishments.

- Trained a team of fifteen new staff members
- Lift up to 50 pounds
- Presented marketing plans to an audience of sixty students
- Managed over thirty events with budgets up to $100,000

Numbers stand out on resumes and in our minds. Using them where appropriate will help employers remember your resume and by extension you.

4. Work Experience or / and Volunteer Experience
List your work experience in chronological order starting with the most recent work experience you had. Since you are listing past experience all the verbs need to be in the past tense. This seems obvious but it is a surprisingly common mistake.

It should look like this:

Job title (position)
Company's name, City, Province

- Use numbers to make your resume stand out
- Focus on achievements

5. Education and training

When including your educational history, use a similar structure to what you used for your Work History when listing your relevant education and training:

Course Name Certificate

School Name, City, Province

Over Qualified / Under Qualified?

Just as with work experience and soft skills, you need to be careful with what you put on your resume.

Let's imagine this scenario. You have a Master's Degree from a different country and decide to apply for an entry level customer service job to get Canadian experience and pay your bills. When you build your resume you list your Master's Degree as part of your education. Six months later you are still applying online and waiting for a response. But still, no one is calling.

Put yourself in the employer's shoes.
Employers want to hire somebody suitable for the job and they are afraid that you might not stay for a long time in that role and eventually they will lose time and money if they hire you and leave shortly after.

When you list your Master' Degree and apply for an entry level job it can be interpreted that you are overqualified for that position. If you really need a job right away, you need to list just what is relevant for that position.

I wish somebody told me that when I start applying for jobs. Focus on the skills and qualifications employers are seeking and tailor all the job search tools you have: resume, cover letter, LinkedIn, blog or website, interviews.

In writing your resume, honesty is extremely important. While you do not want to sell yourself short, you must not lie in your description of self.

One thing that you don't want to communicate to the employer is to sound fake, not genuine, arrogant or not capable.

Resume Checklist
Before sending your resume you want to make sure that you go through this checklist

- Use a name that is easy to be pronounced
- Create an email address specifically for your job search e.g.yourname@gmail.com
- Eliminate the objective and replace it with a personal branding statement or Professional Profile: e.g. Diligent Administrative Assistant; Visionary Junior Architect
- Does your resume look professional and pleasing to the eye?
- Target your resume: A generic resume is a bad idea
- Don't make your resume too long: one or two pages and exception for senior executives or academia
- Don't include "References Available Upon Request"
- Avoid listing hobbies and interests on your resume
- Proofread your resume and avoid errors

Resume Sample

Sarah Johns

your@email.com	xxx-xxx-xxxx	Linked-in Profile

Summary of Qualifications

- **Retail Merchandising Coordinator** with 15+ years of expertise in increasing sales
  through effective merchandising and increased exposure
- Nonviolent Crisis Intervention Certificate; Effective Communication Tools Course
- Strong background in complex problem solving, conflict resolution and negotiation
- Excellent organizational skills; able to prioritize and complete tasks on schedule
- Flexible, understand the need to change and respond to change in a positive manner
- Take initiative in contributing to the team by finding ways to assist others
- Languages: English and Hindi

Areas of Expertise

Leadership
- Promoted to Retail Coordinator after 6 months of employment
- Established solution-based initiatives to solidify processes and procedures
- Trained and coached over 200 Junior Sales Associates

Customer Service / Sales
- Friendly and approachable; greeted customers with courtesy and professionalism
- Performed operational analysis and recommended changes to increase efficiency
- Helped scale successive retail efforts by sharing best practices
- De-escalated customers' complaints ensuring future business and customer satisfaction

Professional Work History

Retail Coordinator / Customer Service Representative   2000 - 2015
SafeWorld, Edmonton, AB

Bank Teller   1999
Financial Ltd., India

Education

Public Relations Diploma - completed first year   2014
University of Alberta, Edmonton, AB
- Courses: Effective Communication Tools, Social Media for Public Relations

Affiliations: Toastmasters
- Mentored 15 members in public speaking and leadership skills development

Resume Online Resources

My Perfect Resume   https://www.myperfectresume.com/

Live Career   https://www.livecareer.com

Resume Dictionary   http://www.resumedictionary.com/

GCF Learn Free   http://www.gcflearnfree.org/career

Cover Letter

What is the purpose of a COVER LETTER?

A cover letter is sent with a resume to make a personal connection with the employer.

It accomplishes this by:

- Leading into the resume
- Answering the question: Why you think you are uniquely qualified and how you would benefit the employer
- Leaving a positive impression

Just like a resume, a cover letter needs to be targeted. Everything on the cover letter needs to support the job objective:

- Read the whole job posting and understand exactly what the employer is looking for
- Highlight the key requirements, skills and experience they want and you have
- Write your letter emphasizing your qualifications in the areas they mentioned
- If employers ask for qualifications you do not have, do not mention them in your letter

Cover Letter Format

Name
City, Province
Phone Number / Email Address

Date

Employer Contact Information (if you have it)
Name, Title
Company
Address, City, Province, Postal Code

RE: Job Title

Dear Mr./Ms. Last Name,

Introduction: 2, 3 sentences that lead into the body of the cover letter. Why are you applying to this position and how do you fit/ match their requirements?

Body: Explain 2-3 key skills, qualifications, achievements that make you the best candidate for the position you are applying for. What do you have to offer the employer? Employers will be more interested in what you can do for them, than a list of your background and is better to make the connection between your qualifications and the job requirements clear.

You can use

1. Paragraph Style or
2. Bullet Style

Conclusion: Conclude your cover letter with 2, 3 sentences where you thank the employer for considering you for the position. Optionally, you can briefly restate why you would be a good fit for the position.
You can also initiate future contact by letting the employer know you will contact them in 3-5 days to follow-up.

Sincerely,

Your full name / Signature

TIPS:
- Keep it short and simple
- Don't make excuses about lacking credentials or experience
- Use bullet points to make it more structured
- Don't copy and paste from your resume

Chapter 7 - Network and Be Visible

Step number 7 is the most powerful step.

The most successful immigrants I met found work before coming here or a week after their arrival in Canada. They already had a network before coming to Canada and they knew how to benefit from it.

Not everyone has relatives or friends already here though. For those who arrive on their own, setting up a network will be difficult, but not impossible. There are still plenty of options.

- Join any community, church, volunteer organization that helps you to connect with people
- Attend a Meetup, Facebook Group and network with people who you share a common interest
- Take a course, program or attend a job club in your employment center

It is not because they necessarily had an awesome resume, knew great job search techniques, or memorized a sell yourself speech. All they had was somebody who was willing to help them.

Establishing a network is not as hard as it sounds. Most people already have one without realizing it.

Networks are composed of people all around us, such as:

How to Crack the 'Hidden' Job Market

What is the Hidden Job Market? It is the way employers prefer filling vacancies.

80% of the jobs are never advertised.

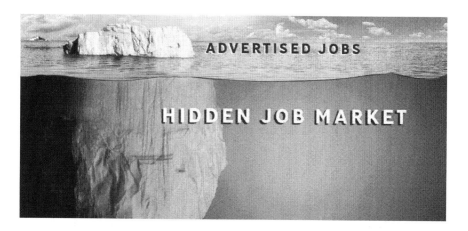

Employers will look for suitable candidates first internally, then they will use their network to get referrals, and they will consider the candidates who proactively initiated the first contact.

When you apply online you focus on 20% of the job opportunities, leftovers after employers didn't find inside what they were looking for.

After six months of intense job searching, plus all the internal and external changes that are happening once you try to integrate yourself in a new environment, you might feel drained and discouraged. Networking will help you speed up the hiring process.

Lou Adler, CEO and founder of The Adler Group came up with this smart formula to improve your odds in finding a job you want.

20-20-60 Job Hunting Program

"-Spend 20% of your time looking for jobs it's obvious you're fully qualified to handle. New tools are being developed that automatically screen resumes based on skills, experiences, track record and the quality of companies worked at and schools attended. That's why the chance of getting a job by applying is so low.

-Spend 20% of your time making sure your resume and LinkedIn profile can be found. Recruiters search for candidates based on their skills, academic backgrounds and special achievements and honors. If you can't be found, you're losing a better chance at getting a job than applying directly.

-Spend 60% of your networking on being creative to get interviewed for jobs you're fully qualified to handle but it's not obvious based on your resume. When you find a job of interest use the backdoor to get an interview rather than applying directly. "

Six Ways to Find those Hidden Jobs

1. Ask

Most people don't ask other people if they know about work opportunities. Either they are shy, or they don't think the other person can help because they are not working in the same industry. Wrong! Anyone can help, anyone can be your network. Even if they don't help directly by recommending you a job, they can recommend you to somebody else.

A while ago I met accidentally with an ex colleague and he told me he lost his job a couple months before and he was still looking for work. I felt bad because we just hired somebody else a week before and I wished he had told me before because I would have tried to help him.

The point is that getting over your natural shyness or pride and asking for help gets more people working on solving your problem.

In contrast, one of my clients posted on her Facebook that she is looking for work and the next day got more than ten job leads from her friends.

2. Informational Interviews

People usually like to talk about their work and successes, especially if they enjoy what they do. Work represents a big chunk of our life. If you meet new people every day and have conversations about what do they do, ask them what they like about their jobs.

You may find they are willing to share useful insights that you would never learn from external sources.

A very effective way to connect with professionals in your industry is through informational interviews. I had no clue about this strategy until I arrived in Canada. If you don't like to call them informational interviews you can call them networking interviews.

Informational interviews are meetings in which job seekers ask for career advice from people who are already in the field they are interested in. You can ask information about the company, the role they have, challenges and unique opportunities associated with that line of work.

It is a very powerful tool because it gives you an opportunity to connect with employers and build a network without asking for a job.

Informational interviews can provide inside information on the job and connect you with the real world.

A very common way to use informational interviews is when you are changing your career. If you decide to start a new career path in Canada, informational interviews will be your best friend. This is how you are going to find out what to do to get where you want.

Before jumping in and taking the road of a new career path, take out a huge loan, invest your energy and time; make sure that you talk with people from the field that you are interested in and ask them for advice. No one knows better than them what exactly it means to do that job.

It might give you another perspective and bring clarity in your search

When I met one of my case managers I asked her what her job was about, what were her job duties, challenges, and opportunities in that field. She gave so many leads and recommendations that I was shocked that I got so much insight from one simple question. In fact, because we had that conversation and she was so inspiring I decided to follow her path and enroll in an educational program.

How to set up an informational interview:

> The first step is to make a list of companies you would love to work at and positions you'd be interested in.

> Second is to find information regarding the people who are working there. Most companies have a website,

phone, email address, LinkedIn account where you can contact and ask for help.

➢ Third is to develop a considerate email that gets right to the point:

"Dear Mr. Miller,

I found your name and contact information on Marketing Professional Group Network. Given the fact you have over five years of experience in the marketing field I would appreciate the chance to ask you a few questions and pick your brain about your experience.

If you would be willing to have a conversation by email, Skype or phone, I would be incredibly grateful.

Thank you very much in advance for your time and insight.

Alison Smith "

When you go to Informational Interviews make sure that you are prepared with a set of questions.

You might ask:

1. What is your job like?

2. What kind of problems do you deal with?

3. Why did this type of work interest you, and how did you get started?

4. How did you get your job? What jobs and experiences have led you to your present position?

5. What are the most important satisfactions and dissatisfactions connected with your occupation?

6. What are the various jobs in this field or organization?

7. Which schools offer courses or training for the job?

TIP: In informational interviews you have to think about two components: a personal and a professional one. Yes, you want to make a connection and build your network and hope that this will lead you to a future job but don't forget that people can sense if you are genuine and really interested in knowing more about them.

I heard people telling me that didn't work for them very well and this is because most of the time they focus on what they can get from the person who gives the information and are not interested about their personal and professional experience.

3. Volunteer

Volunteering is the perfect tool to discover or develop new skills, connect with the world and reach out to the community.

If you are worried about Canadian experience, an easy way to get that experience is to join an organization that you believe in and you would like to contribute. Canada is the right country to volunteer. Thousands of non-profits, charities covering a whole range of missions and trying to help and solve problems in the communities.

Benefits:

- Canadian experience
- Get to meet people and build your network

- Gain relevant skills
- Have additional relevant information to add in your resume
- Employers will appreciate you for your values and that you are willing to give your time to help
- You will have more self-confidence because giving will empower you

Here are some of the well-known websites:

Charity Village - http://charityvillage.com/

Go Volunteer - http://www.govolunteer.ca/

Volunteer Canada https://volunteer.ca/

"One of the great ironies of life is this: He or she who serves almost always benefits more than he or she who is served." – Gordon Hinckle

4. Meetup

Meetup is the "world's largest network of local groups".

Meetup makes it easy for people who have a similar interest to connect. There are groups of people who are there for the same reason and want to share, network, teach, help or make new friends.

It gives you the possibility to make new contacts and get the motivation and support to move forward.

I am personally a big fan of Meetup. This is how I started building my network and it has helped many new immigrants in Canada.

Meetup: http://www.meetup.com/

5. Facebook

Facebook can be great for family and friends but also when you look for work. It can help even more if you have an established network here. Be careful to delete all the bad pictures from your profile or change the privacy settings.

Employers will commonly screen applicants by goggling their name to see if there is any public information about the applicant that will present a problem. So goggle your name and see what comes up!

Facebook: https://www.facebook.com/

6. LinkedIn

LinkedIn is the most powerful online tool for professional networking. It is similar to posting your resume online on a website but at the same time providing the possibility to be transparent and connect with ex colleagues, companies, employers. And it's perfect for showing off your experience and skills.

Make sure you come across professionally and use correct grammar and spelling, build a powerful profile and connect with professionals in your field and from Canada.

LinkedIn: https://www.linkedin.com/uas/login

How to use LinkedIn at its full potential

- Create a clear plan on what you are looking to achieve from the platform

- Connect with as many people and companies in your field as possible

- Focus on building relationships - endorse people for their skills; offer testimonials about their services or performance on the job

- Send personalized messages to people who you are aiming to connect with

- Keep an eye on who's viewed your profile and send back an invitation

Did you know?
- Facebook has over a billion accounts and LinkedIn has over 414 million users and it is growing
- 94% of recruiters use LinkedIn for screening candidates

7. Create Your Business Card

Networking can happen anywhere and anytime so you better be prepared for any situation. One simple way to connect and stay in touch with people you have just met is to have your business card.

If you wonder what I am talking about since you might not have a business yet, I am referring to a "calling card" which can be used for casual situations where a resume might be inappropriate and is a great way to tell people about your skills and experience in a couple words.

What To Include On The Card?

Contact information

- Your name
- Phone number
- Email address

Job objective / Personal branding statement

- Experienced Career Coached
- Visionary Junior Architect

Work Experience & Education / Training related to the job objective

- 2 - 3 key skills

Business Card Sample

How to expand your network:

The more people you are going to know the more chances to find work you will have, in North America more than 80% of the people find work through networking:

- Personal network

- Volunteer

- Informational interviews

- Be open to meet new people everywhere - face-to-face contacts

- Call employers (targeted)

- Networking meetings and industry events

- Join a Meetup

- Social media: LinkedIn, Facebook

From weakness to strength

We all have our unique stories and when looking for work there are different factors that influence our success: age, education, occupation, skills, ethnicity and the list goes on.

There are things that we can control and things that we can't.

It is pointless to focus on what we can't change because blaming the government or system will not make your situation easier. On the contrary, I met immigrants who struggled for a while in Canada and now they are bitter about the system, lost trust in people and are nostalgic about their home countries.

If you decided to stay here and you have a drive for success, then stop any negativity right now. The most important personality trait that will help you to keep going is your positive attitude. This will allow you to turn your struggle into strength.

Many immigrants I talked with feel disadvantaged because they don't speak perfect English, are lacking Canadian experience or a social and professional network. But if we change our perspective we can transform all the weaknesses into strengths.

First of all, Canada is a land of immigrants and a mosaic of cultures. This is how this country was built. The latest Canada Census figures suggest that "One in five speaks a foreign language at home."

Even thought English and French are the official languages and you need to have a good English or French level to be able to get and perform on the job, people who are hiring you; your future colleagues, your clients are most probably going to speak a second language. Being an immigrant and speaking a second language can be a great asset that you can use in any job.

The second point is that Canadian qualifications or Canadian experience is something that most immigrants will get in the first couple months after their arrival. Whether you start your credential recognition process, take a course, volunteer for your community, get an internship, or find an entry level job it is still Canadian experience.

And last, networking, is the most important competitive advantage those others can have.

Everyone can become an effective networker! This is no hocus pocus or magic! It is learning "how to" and "apply it".

One of my first steps after I moved here was to connect with as many people possible. After three years of living in Canada, I can say that I have a bigger network of people than I had back home.

Nothing is possible without the help of others.

Chapter 8 - Conduct a Successful Job Search

Even if you decide to apply online remember about the Hidden Job Market – jobs postings represent only 20% of available jobs. 80% of jobs are not posted.

Use 80% of your time to network and connect with companies and people directly to find "hidden" jobs. Before applying online make sure you have a targeted resume and cover letter.

There are 3 types of Online Job Applications

1. By Email - If replying to job postings

2. Job Search website- Uploading your resume

3. Company website - If you have targeted a particular company

Top 10 Best Job Websites in Canada

- ➢ Indeed.com
- ➢ Monster
- ➢ GlassDoor
- ➢ Craigslist
- ➢ Simply Hired

- Eluta
- CareerBuilder
- Job Bank
- LinkedIn
- Workopolis

TIP: When you apply online try different keywords

- Job Title
- Expertise (CRM, QuickBooks,)
- Education / Qualifications (First Aid, Forklift)
- Location (Vancouver)
- Language (French, Mandarin, Punjabi, Bilingual)

Chapter 9 - Winning the Interviews

The whole interview process can be long and draining. Even if you have a professional resume and cover letter that say everything about your work experience and skills, employers still want to meet you in person.

Why?

To get to know you. A resume is just a document (not legal) and the reality can be quite different. You can write in your resume that you have a "positive attitude" and "excellent customer service skills" but when you present yourself in an interview you shake, fidget, don't smile, avoid eye contact and you can't clearly articulate your ideas.

The most important thing that you can work at is your first impression. They will judge you and make a hiring decision in less than five seconds on how you look, how you are dressed, how you smell, how you are looking at them, what kind of energy you convey. And after that you can focus on answering questions!

The most common types of interviews are:

- Telephone interview (pre-screening)

- 1-2-1 Interview

- Panel Interview - more than one interviewer

- Group Interview - multiple candidates interviewed at the same time

- Video interview - Skype, FaceTime

How to win interviews

Before the interview

➢ Research the company - Why do you want to work for them?
➢ Ask for names of interviewers
➢ Prepare questions to ask the interviewer

During the interview

➢ Arrive ten minutes early, not more
➢ First impression – Firm handshake, eye contact and smile
➢ Listen, identify primary concerns and formulate answers
➢ Use SAR model for behavioural questions

3 Types of Questions to Expect

- Classical questions: Tell me about yourself, what are your strengths, weaknesses?

- Behavioral questions: Tell me about a time you had a conflict at work?

- Situational questions: What would you do if a client starts yelling at you?

There are many possible questions that you can prepare for but I will talk only about the most common

1. Tell me about yourself?

It's normally at the beginning of the interview. If you are like me you might smile, relax and start talking about your family, where are you from, when you came to Canada.

But unfortunately this is not what the employer cares about.

All they want to know is about your professional background.

Here is a simple structure to follow.

Note how similar it is to how you construct a resume.

Profile

+

How are you going to fix my problem?

Name: My name is Joy (first name only).

Work: I have more than five years of experience as a Workshop Facilitator and Career Coach

Education: I am a certified Career Development Practitioner

Hard Skills: I have a strong background in resume and cover letter development and facilitated more than 300 job search workshops.

Optional:

Soft Skills: I listen carefully when people talk and develop authentic relationships

Achievements: Recognized for putting clients at ease and for having perfect attendance

Languages: Fluent in English, Spanish and French

The same structure can be used as an "Elevator Speech" for any cold-calling and self-marketing in online profiles.

2. What are your strengths?

Employers want to know all your positive qualities. But, just like soft skills, you can't just list them off. It is more about telling a story that demonstrates your unique strengths.

Research what kind of person suits the job you are applying for. What are the skills and strengths related to the job? You already have a list of the top soft skills most wanted by employers.

Focus on three main skills relevant to the job that also reflect your personality and use examples that illustrate those skills.

Example:

Showing initiative – In my previous job I was acknowledged by my supervisor and colleagues for always taking initiative. If I see something that needs to be done, I don't wait for instruction, I just do it.

3. What are your weaknesses?

Never say something like: "I work too hard" or "I am a perfectionist". Employers might think you are not realistic and don't have self-awareness. However, they don't want you to say: I don't have any weakness!

The truth is that everyone has weaknesses and everyone knows it. But that doesn't mean the employer actually wants to hear about yours. Even if they ask.

One tip I learned from Toastmasters that helped me in my interviews: Don't respond directly to their questions by actually listing off your weaknesses.

It is more powerful to mention what you are working to improve. You can start with "one area that I could strengthen" or "one area that I could develop".

E.g. "One area I could strengthen is my English. Since I came to Canada I joined a Toastmasters club and completed my Effective Communicator Manual. Also I have been studying grammar and improving my vocabulary in my own time."

4. What do you know about us?

As a job seeker who wants to stand out from the crowed you need to do your due diligence and find out about the company before your interview. Always research the company before your interview, and if they have a website read about their mission, values or policies. This preparation will demonstrate your interest in the job.

Sample answer, based on research:

"Based on my research I know that is a leader in the field of [whatever field they lead] and I want to work for an employer I can be proud of"

You can look for new programs and projects; products or services offered by the company, their mission and how they describe themselves.

If you want to find insides about the company use Glassdoor.ca. and check out staff, Board members and reviews about the company.

5. What are your goals for the next 5 years?

No interviewer expects you to know exactly what you will be doing in 1,825 days.

Employers want to know more about your career goals and how this position would fit into your life as you are more likely to perform well and stick around if this position is important for you and your future.

A simple answer can be:

"My long-term goals involve growing with a company where I can continue to learn, take on additional responsibilities, and contribute as much of value as I can. But most importantly, I want to work for an organization where I can build a career"

6. Tell me about a time you had a conflict at work?

Employers ask these questions because past behaviour can predict future performance. For any behavioural question you can use the Situation Action Result (SAR) model.

S – Situation

A – Action

R – Result

This structure gives you the possibility to tell a story about yourself. It is much more powerful than just listing some adjectives about how good at conflicts you are!

The first rule is - give them a great story!

Situation: Describe a specific situation or task that you needed to accomplish or resolve. You can include names, dates and places but don't lose yourself in too many details!

Action: What was the action you took? What did you do you to fix the situation?

Result: What kind of result did you have? Explain how your clients, colleagues, and employers benefited by your actions and end your story on a positive note.

It is best not memorize your SAR story. Rather, practice telling your story aloud, alone or with your spouse. This way you will not sound robotic and will help you to keep the stories fresh in your mind.

Most common Behavioral Question:

- ✓ Tell me about a time when you were faced with a stressful situation?
- ✓ Tell me about a time when you missed a deadline?
- ✓ Tell me about a time when you demonstrated time management skills?
- ✓ Give me an example when you showed initiative in the workplace?
- ✓ Give me an example when you failed to achieve your goals?
- ✓ Tell me about a time when you motivated others?

✓ Give me an example when you had to use your persuasion skills to influence someone's opinion?

✓ Give me an example when you worked in a team to achieve a common goal?

7. Do you have any questions?

Employers aren't interested in a candidate who isn't really interested in them or the job they are applying for. Also an interview is a two-way street, you can use questions to find out about the position and the company or staff working there in order to make a decision if you want to work for them or not.

You must be prepared at least with three questions that demonstrate your interested in the position.

Sample Questions:

What do you think are the most important qualities for someone to excel in this role?

Is there any additional information that I can provide about my qualification?

What is the company culture?

Can you describe what are the biggest challenges facing the company?

What are the next steps in the hiring process?

Can I follow up in the next couple days?

One advantage about interviews in North America is that 80% of the questions will always be the same; so you can develop interview skills through practice and self reflection.

Mistakes you should avoid in interviews

- ➢ Do not come late or too early- arrive 15 minutes before the interview
- ➢ Never mention any negative experiences of past employees
- ➢ Do not act like you know everything
- ➢ Don't ask in your first interview about salary or benefits
- ➢ Avoid negative, weak or imperative words like: no, I can't, I don't, I disagree, I have a strong opinion, you should / shouldn't,

After the interview

- ➢ Relax, you survived!

- ➢ Write down Positive moments and Improvements to be made
- ➢ Send a thank you email / letter (after 24 hours)

"Remember, it always seems impossible until it's done"

Chapter 10 - Negotiate, Close the Deal and Build Trust

Most of the time at the end of the interview you are asked this question:

What are your salary requirements?

This question is designed to screen you out!

If they didn't mention the hourly pay in the job posting, expect to have this type of question. But remember, don't be the first one to ask the question. The makes it seem like your focus will be on what you can get and not on what you can give.

First of all, when you do your research you need to know how much money you can get in your field of expertise. There are many ways you can find about it.

PayScale, Salary.com and Glassdoor are great tools to research salary information matched to your exact job profile and company reviews from former employees.

Never discuss the salary until you are offered the job and you are absolutely sure that they want to hire you.

If you are asked this question though, the first rule is to try to defer it:

"I really need more information about the job requirements and expectations before I can formulate my answer"

And if you can't defer it:

"Based on my research, with my experience and qualifications, the salary range appears to be in the $55–$60,000. Is that a range that fits with your compensation structure?"

Before they sign the contract and hire you, the employer will check your references. This can be an obstacle for people who are looking for their first job in Canada.

Who can be your reference?

- Supervisor, manager

- Colleagues, other business partners

- Clients, customers who you worked with

- Volunteer organizations

- Instructors, program coordinators

- Mentors

The most important thing is that a reference be positive. Whether in a letter, an email or a phone call your reference needs to talk about you in a positive light. They need to acknowledge you for your strengths, values and how you were you able to provide value in the organization you have worked for.

Employers will also check references from your home country. Unless you make it easy for them, this could become a problem.

What you need to provide:

- ➢ Reference's name
- ➢ Position in the company
- ➢ Company Name
- ➢ Email address / Phone
- ➢ Mention if it is in a different time zone

Building a Solid Reputation

Now you've got your first job in Canada!

How are you going to maintain it? How are you going to advance in your career?

It time for you to do what you said you are going to do!

Everything is reflected through our values. If you say you have integrity and the very next day you are late, your behaviour is not consistent. If you often call in sick you don't prove you are reliable. This is why employers are so careful when screening candidates for a job.

Getting the job doesn't mean that your contract will be extended after three months of probation. Employers can terminate your contract during that time. In fact, many employees don't last to long in a new position. Why?

Here are the most common reasons why new employees don't last:

- They are lacking motivation and drive to succeed
- They are unable to accept feedback
- Their technical skills are inadequate for the job
- Their attitude isn't suited to the job
- They talk bad about their last boss

- They aren't a good fit

Your values will be your compass in life. Depending on what sort of values you demonstrate, they will advance you or get you in trouble.

> Employers want to trust you. They will give you money, a company car, a computer, and any other benefits that will come with the job. They expect you to perform and be the person you promised to be.

- ➤ They want you to be on time. Punctuality is highly valued by employers. You may come from a culture where time isn't regarded so highly, but in Canada, time is extremely important.

- ➤ They want you to be flexible. Job requirements are changing all the time. You are hired to do one thing but shortly after the job can change unexpectedly. Employers will ask you to do more with less, to change work hours, to work overtime, to take on new responsibilities, to train others.

- ➤ They will expect you to be positive. Everyone is attracted to positive and happy people. Even if you are lacking some skills and qualifications employers will be more likely to hire you because of your energy and enthusiasm that you bring to the job. Be open to feedback.

Everyone makes mistakes when it comes to their jobs. Nobody is perfect. But be ready to learn from your mistakes.

Out of the box tips:

- 50 - 50 rule: if you want to be successful in interviews focus 50% of your time listening and 50% of your time speaking

- Avoid over talking: be clear and to the point when you answer interview questions. You will have the interviewer's attention for no more than 90 sec

- Dress for success. Research the company you are interested in working for and find out how they are dressing at work. At your interview dress a level higher than they normally wear at work.

- Always focus on what you can give and how you can help. Show empathy and listen to what people have to say. If they have a problem and you think you can help, simply ask: "How can I help you?" Giving is the best way to communicate.

- When somebody asks you what you are doing now, you can also say: "I am between successes."

Conclusion

My mission has been to equip you with the most important job searching tools so you can thrive in a new culture in the shortest time possible.

Every new immigrant to Canada comes with dreams, hopes and a possibility of having a great job and an amazing life. There will always be difficult situations, obstacles and fears to overcome. I've had many people tell me "No" and "it is impossible" and "you can't make it" in my life.

But once I learned the principles and techniques that I have shared with you in this guide, I've found that I can climb as high as I want to go.

By following these ten easy steps you will be fully prepared to start searching for and get hired in a great job even before you set foot on Canadian soil, positioning you for success.

Download your FREE Special Gift!

Thank you for purchasing my eBook "10 Steps to Find Work and Be Successful in Canada"

My free gift for you: **Best Resume Templates and Tips**

I want to share with you my best Resume Templates and Resume Tips I use for designing a resume that stands out and get interviews. These templates work like a charm, and I'm giving them to you for free, just because I want to see you succeed!

Copy into your browser the following link:

https://forms.aweber.com/form/23/2018776223.htm

Happy job hunting!

Disclaimer

While all attempts have been made to verify the information
provided in this book, the author does not assume any responsibility
for errors, omissions, or contrary interpretations of the subject
matter contained within. The information provided in this book is
for educational and entertainment purposes only. The reader is
responsible for his or her own actions and the author does not
accept any responsibilities for any liabilities or damages, real or
perceived, resulting from the use of this information.

23892630R00058

Printed in Great Britain
by Amazon